How to Heal
A BROKEN
Heart

TRANSITION FROM PAIN TO PEACE

SARITA A. FOXWORTH

Printed in the United States of America

2 3 4 5 6 7 8 9 10

ISBN 978-1985161498 (Paperback Edition)

ISBN 978-0692118337 (Hardcover Edition)

Published by The Single Woman's Bookstore

www.thesinglewomansbookstore.com

Contents

Introduction

TIME DOES NOT HEAL. JESUS DOES.

Isaiah 61:1

The Spirit of the Lord God is upon Me, because the Lord has anointed Me to preach good tidings to the poor; He has sent Me to [a]heal the brokenhearted, to proclaim liberty to the captives, and the opening of the prison to those who are bound.

Jesus is our Mender of Broken Hearts, our Healer. We have heard this, we read the Bible stories and may have even studied about healing in great depth. However, it seems as if when our heart is broken we struggle with our own inner spiritual healing. Peace and strength allude us. Try as we may, we just can't seem to get past the hurt. The pain seems unbearable and thoughts of regret, guilt, and memories of what went wrong plagues our mind/emotions every second of every day. We pray and study the Word, and feel good in the moment. We believe

1

we have our joy back but as the day turns to night, the pain seems to consume every fiber of our being.

I understand this all too well. I understand how we can know that Jesus is our Healer, and yet struggle with that truth becoming our reality. We feel as if our prayers are hitting the ceiling. We may even hear God saying, I love you, I got you, and I will take care of you...yet our heart still hurts. We can't seem to gain regular, consistent and lasting peace.

The path to healing I have outlined in this book can and will get you to a place of real, lasting peace and joy. You will receive your healing permanently if you follow the practical application given. Repeat the application as often as you need to. I do not believe God wants us to take years to heal. He wants us to get on with our lives and fulfill his plans and purpose. He wants us whole and not wearing a mask of happiness while we feel as though we are still dying on the inside.

The old saying is that "Time heals all wounds". I do not believe that statement to be a fact. The fact is that Jesus is our Healer. When we read the synoptic gospels, there is not an example where Jesus lays hands on the sick or broken and then tells them to go and allow time to do the rest. That is because there is no power in time. Time is a tool to guide us in life; it is not what heals us. While we do need to take things one day at a time and not live in the past or worry about our future, that does not mean we should wait on time to heal our hearts.

When Jesus healed the woman with the issue of blood, she left his presence whole. She did not leave waiting on the manifestation of what her faith demanded. I believe that just as this woman left his presence whole, we too can have an encounter with Christ and leave whole. When I began the journey of healing my broken heart, I received healing fairly quickly. It was a rough process because of the shock of being cheated on and the guilt of breaking my own relationship rules. Yet, I was determined to not live in that place of hurt and brokenness. I was determined to get my healing from God and move on with my life.

How do we manifest permanent and total healing? We make a very conscience decision to choose not to stay stuck in brokenness, but to move forward in Christ. As a woman of God, you have the Spirit of God living on the inside of you. You already possess the full magnitude of Christ's power and glory. The same Jesus that healed the woman with the issue of blood is living within your spirit. The same power that made her whole immediately, you have direct access to that same power right now.

Healing does not require time. It requires faith and trust in God alone. We have access to every single promise God made us through our faith. He is not a powerless, weak God. You are not a powerless weak woman. You are a woman of strength and a woman of power. Access this inward strength and power through your faith. Take from God what you need right now. You need immediate deliverance and healing. You need to get your emotions under control. You need to get back to your place of peace and reignite your belief that the man God has for you will soon come. Place all your energy and focus on the things above. Allow Jesus to heal you. There is no promise that time will heal us. Jehovah Rapha is our great God, who heals us through the Holy Spirit of Jesus Christ that lives within us.

PART 1

For the Sake of Love

DECEIVED AND BACKSLIDDEN

Chapter 1

HEARTBREAKING CONVERSATIONS

Jeremiah 33:3 New King James Version (NKJV)

Call to Me, and I will answer you, and show you great and mighty things, which you do not know.

The Lord will reveal all things in time. As his precious daughters, we can pray and ask that he reveal a man's character, intentions, and heart so that we may make the right decisions. Because he wants the best for you and he wants you walking in wisdom, he will answer your heart's cry quickly. The night before the following conversation took place, I prayed and asked God to reveal all things that I could not see. When you pray for this in your own life, the revelation he gives can lead you into a place of great blessing and peace, or it can force you to make hard decisions which will ultimately be in line with God's will for your life even if it hurts presently. Be prepared to accept, listen and obey. Remember, all things are working together for your good.

A CONVERSATION WITH THE SIDE CHICK

I could not believe what I was hearing. My ear was glued to the phone listening intently as my man begged his side chick to listen to him, and not to believe a word I was saying. I heard him plead with her to please talk to him and hang up the phone on me. I heard her telling him to stop touching her and get away. I heard him ask her "But who am I with, who am I with though?" At her request, I texted her several screen shots of him telling me he loved me. She needed proof that I wasn't lying. When they put me on speaker phone, I asked him, "Didn't you tell me you loved me?" I heard him yell "NO!".

The truth was that we had been together for several months. When I found out about this woman, I saw that she was pregnant and thought maybe she was his main woman and I was the side chick all along. But, no, I was wrong. As we talked more I found out they had only been together a few weeks, so she was pregnant with another man's child. I was with him less than two weeks prior to this phone conversation. He was in my bed, singing to me, telling me he loved me and wrapping his arms all around me. So, I am not sure exactly when their love affair started. I also know that even though I brought light to myself so that I could gain the truth, they are still together to this day.

I never imagined that a sensible woman of God would stay with a man who had been cheating on his girlfriend and her at the same time. He lied to both of us. Even though I heard her yell at him, I could tell by her tone of voice that she would stay with him. I could tell when two hours later she was still texting me saying he was still there lying and asking me for more screen shots. She needed more proof. Apparently, my actual existence and what I already sent to her was not enough. I did not send her anything else. I knew it didn't matter what else I could have sent to her because she wanted to believe him.

Chapter 1

What she really wanted from me was a reason to stay with him. I didn't blame her though. I didn't judge my sister. I understood her situation. Her desire for love and support especially while pregnant and having an absent baby's father is greater than the reality of getting fake love versus no love at all.

FAKE LOVE VERSUS NO LOVE

I have taken fake love instead of no love before myself. The relationship I developed with this man, John, was fake love. Fake love feels so good in the moment. It's warm, it's kind, it's fun, and it fulfills a need, albeit a temporary need. However, fake love is missing some components that differentiate it from real love. The consistency, longevity, purity, selflessness, and peace that comes from real love cannot be found in fake love. Fake love comes to fill you up, then leaves you empty. Fake love deceives you. Most times it leaves you with questions, hurt, anxiety, fear, and insecurity. It leaves you unsure of yourself or the person who claims to love you.

How to Heal a Broken Heart

A CONVERSATION WITH THE HEARTBREAKER

The next day I received nonstop phone calls from John which I didn't answer, but I did respond with text messages. I used words that I didn't even know existed in my vocabulary anymore. Words that I hadn't use since my supernatural encounter with Christ 9 years prior. I called him every name and wished every curse upon his life. My heart was completely broken. That was the immediate manifestation of my rage. I prayed in the midst of pain and confusion. However, my flesh was out of control. My mind and heart were being tormented. I asked him why he cheated on me. He said it was because he felt like he didn't deserve me. He wasn't as financially established as I was. He said I pushed him away. I knew that was a lame excuse. A real man doesn't run into another woman's bed because he suddenly realizes he needs to step it up. A real man loves a successful, ambitious woman because he recognizes that as value and not as something to make him look down upon himself. A real man wouldn't claim a woman pushed him away because she required loyalty and honesty. A real man doesn't live a fabricated life. I realized I was not dealing with a real man, but a boy. I do not say this from a place of anger towards him. This statement is based on the biblical principle of knowing a tree by its fruit. He did not bear the fruits of a mature man of God, in more than this area alone, which we will discuss later.

THE AFTERMATH: FROM PAIN TO PEACE

I was so hurt, I cried and cried. I called out from work the next day because my mind couldn't focus. However, I knew that God was still with me and that my Heavenly Father had my answers and my healing. Even when my mouth was on fire with cursing and slander, I still prayed. I prayed in the Spirit, and I

Chapter 1

prayed in English. I listened to a powerful sermon about sexual wholeness, because yes, I had broken my celibacy walk. I read a life transforming book about being delivered and healed from offense and hurt. I talked it over with another man of God who gave me the best advice. I kept praying even though pain was screaming louder than God's voice. I blocked John's number and deleted him from my phone. I blocked him on social media. I deleted his side chick's number and all her messages telling me how sorry she was that I was going through this as she had been through a similar situation. These are a few of actions I took, just a brief synopsis of my healing process, but I will go into greater depth and detail throughout the upcoming chapters.

Now, not only am I healed, but I live in a place where I am experiencing the greatest peace of my life. I want to share with you where I was and how I got here today. In this book, I will give 5 powerful ways to heal from a broken heart and permanently move from pain to peace. I will share the details of how I moved forward not only at the end of this relationship, but others with men inside the church, leaders in ministry and also outside of the church.

Although most of the stories do not involve years invested or a broken marriage, I want to encourage you if you happen to be in one of those situations. Take the wisdom, coaching, advice, and testimonies given and apply what you can, where you can in your own life. Be careful not to judge my level of devastation and assume it was not as bad as yours. Heartbreak is heartbreak. Pain in pain. And healing is healing. Do not overcomplicate the process because your situation may seem more complicated. Please hear my heart, sis. Make it as simple as possible, with the leadership of the Holy Spirit. Step by step, day by day. God is not the author of confusion, and he does not want you to complicate your healing. He wants you to simplify the process and receive it, as quickly as possible, as do I. If you have layers of your life intertwined with a man, yes, you do have to begin to untangle your lives and embrace your new singlehood. My focus in this book is practical ways to repair your mental, emotional and heart condition. The Lord will give you grace and wisdom for all the details of your specific situation.

My hope is that through my transparency, I can help you get back to a place of great faith and joy in the Lord Jesus. I don't believe healing should take years or even months in some cases. Jesus is our Healer, not time. You can do this. You can heal, let go of the hurt and pain and move on from the past. You can also gain understanding into the spiritual attack that took place on your soul at the hands of your enemy: Satan. My prayer is that you receive swift and complete healing and deliverance as you work through this book and transform your life.

Chapter 2

THE GOOD DEACON

---

1 John 4:1 New King James Version (NKJV)

Beloved, do not believe every spirit, but test the spirits, whether they are of God; because many false prophets have gone out into the world.

Satan is the great deceiver; he is the father of lies. Some people are being deceived and do not realize they are living in deception by choice. God loves us. He will not allow us to become deceived without warning and clarity. Through the words and influence we allow others to impart into our lives we are subject to deception. We also can deceive ourselves by allowing our desire for marriage to consume our thoughts and lead us to compromise our values and disobey God. Godly conviction and discernment is our protection from deception.

THE GREAT DECEPTION

In order for you to understand my state of mind when I met John, I must first start with my previous relationship with Reggie AKA The Good Deacon. I wasn't fully healed from that relationship when I began dating John.

I met Reggie and John through an online dating website. I believed I heard from God in prayer one night at the beginning of that year that he wanted me to go online to increase my chances of meeting and dating men. I lived a busy and organized life that pretty much consisted of going to work, picking up my one year old and tending to him when I got home. On weekends, I might go to the bookstore, the park or to my parents' house to visit. Other than regular trips to Walmart for groceries, I didn't do anything regularly to meet and possibly date new men. My schedule didn't allow for it. So, I believed I had truly heard from God, that he would send my King through unconventional 21st century means.

I paid for two websites and signed up for another free. There were a plethora of men reaching out to me, and I became not only overwhelmed, but also disappointed in the attributes they presented. They didn't possess the godly and fruitful package I desired in a godly husband, and it was time consuming sifting through hundreds of messages daily. Within two weeks I canceled all the accounts and never had a telephone conversation with any of the men who reached out to me.

Eight months later a friend of mine told me about a dating website I had never heard of. She told me how herself and another coworker were having fun meeting and dating men from the website. These were professional and high quality black women, so I assumed the men were also high quality. That same week I saw a commercial for the website, which ironically, I have not seen since that day. I thought to myself, well if six figure money making women are on the website meeting men, and I see this random commercial advertising the website, I might as well try online dating again. I thought, maybe now was the time and this was the website God wanted me on. I told myself that if I didn't like it, I would simply delete my account just like earlier that year.

It was a warm sunny afternoon as I sat in my living room and the sun poured through my Venetian blinds while my 1-year old baby boy was upstairs napping. I was chilling with my feet up, drinking sweet tea, getting caught up on my favorite powerful-single-woman-drama television series. I was at such a peaceful and restful place in my life. I was spiritually and emotionally whole and having fun focused on the things of God. Each week I worked on decorating and putting my new home in order which I had purchased just a few months prior. I was in a pretty good swing of things as a new single first-time mother. My job as a quality assurance officer was going well, the coaching practice I owned (my side hustle) was flowing, and I was losing the baby weight that I had gained. My baby boy and I had traveled to beaches all summer and hosted barbeques and parties. Things were going really well in my life. So, I decided to sign up on this new dating website after I saw the commercial, I figure I had nothing to lose, and I wouldn't take it too seriously. It would just be something to do, that hopefully would lead to a real connection with someone.

Within hours of signing up, just like the other websites I was flooded with "Hey Beautiful", "How you doing?", "What's up pretty lady?" messages. This time around, I interacted with only the men who showed they had a "relationship" with Jesus in their profile and the first questions I asked pertained to church attendance, using curse words and celibacy until marriage.

I determined these questions would weed out any man who did not know God and who did not live by God's standards. I would later find out; I was wrong.

I started talking regularly on the phone to a deacon of a 7th Day Adventist church. I call him "The Good Deacon" his name was Reggie. What I will share about our relationship in no way represents that entire denomination or how their men act or think. This is simply my experience with him; I share his denomination because I want you to understand the differences between how he worshipped and how I worship. I do not know much about that denomination other than what he shared with me and what I witnessed firsthand when I visited the church. I consider myself a non-denominational follower of Christ. Even though this relationship did not work out, it turned out to be a blessing to me. I realized how impactful one person's lifestyle could be when people are making an interpretation of any religion or belief system. My lesson learned was to be careful how I treat people when I profess Christ and also when I invite them to church. Your lifestyle, behaviors, and actions are speaking as a representative of that religion, belief system or church to that one individual you are communicating or connected with.

When we first started talking, I was so impressed when I asked him what he was doing one Wednesday evening, and he told me he was going to serve in a ministry, clothing and feeding the homeless. I admired him, even more, when he told me how he spent his entire Saturdays at church learning and serving, even after he worked the overnight shift at his job. The more we talked and he told me he didn't watch much TV because of the demonic implications and he mainly listened to a classic old school rapper and sermons, I grew more and more interested in him. When we spoke about prayer and the Word of

Chapter 2

God, I loved his hunger for knowledge and how he could quote and explain scriptures.

So, when this man of God asked me to be in a relationship with him after only a few days of talking and meeting up, I agreed. I felt a connection, but I didn't voice it. He told me how he felt like he could always talk to me all night and how he felt like he had known me forever, even though we had just met. He often told me I was amazing and that I sounded like his future wife. We spent lots of time together over the next coming weeks, and I was having fun with him.

On our first date, I believe I could visually sense his heart. I saw beyond his physical chest, and perceived a great sadness and yearning. I asked him later was he sad about anything and of course, he said no. I prayed about what I saw, and I prayed for his heart. I believe the Lord revealed to me that he still had a great deal of pain and sadness from his divorce 10 years ago, yet at the same time he was yearning for love presently. I was willing to be that person to love him through his pain.

Unfortunately, the more time I spent with him, the more the red flags started to show. I noticed that he did curse, even though when I spoke about another man cursing and talking about God simultaneously he agreed that was wrong. I found out he was not celibate and was indirectly pressuring me to have sex with him. His spiritual beliefs were twisted in error, and he attacked great men of God and the body of Christ as a whole. He also hadn't fully healed from his divorce from 10 years ago which he freely admitted at one point. I also found out he did indulge in carnal music when he started blasting cursing rap music from my Bluetooth speaker at a party I was hosting. Through random comments and corresponding actions, I discerned that he was full of a perverted lust for transgender men and was possibly bisexual himself. However, I did not judge him for any of these things because I understand none of us are perfect people. I myself am always working to become more Christ-like and may do things that others consider carnal or improper as well. Yet and still, these are not traits or characteristics that I desire in a godly husband, for my son to take after, or for my children to look up to as a leader in our home.

YOU ARE NOT TOO PICKY

When your discernment starts to pick up on caution and warning signals, known as red flags, we should take action with the information we are receiving. That action could be to pray for them, bring it to their attention with wisdom and love, or to exit the relationship. At times it could be all three. These red flags could also be a sign that the relationship should not progress pass the friendship phase. I believe discernment is a gift from God to protect his daughters. You are not being too picky if you notice red flags and choose to walk away. You are not being judgmental if you notice a man's character, traits, and lifestyle which are all the fruit of what is in his heart, and you decide those things are not what you want to go into your future. As the fruit on his life is exposed to you, you can make a wise decision on how to move forward with the relationship.

Unfortunately, as the red flags began to unveil themselves over time, I started to have strong feelings for him as well. Reggie was kind, laid back and gentle. We didn't have many disagreements, but when we did, he always said the right things to calm me down and bring resolution quickly. He would fix any issue brought up perfectly and looked me in the eyes with much affection. He would always come visit and want me to tell him what I needed his help with around the house so that he could be the man in my life. He wanted to hang out and do the same types of things I enjoyed doing like going to the beach, hosting cookouts and spending time with family. He brought me around his family and close friends and would tell me many personal details about his divorce. We spent lots of time conversing and hanging out together. He made me feel loved and happy.

EXTERNAL DECEPTION BIRTHS SELF-DECEPTION

My connection to him grew strong, so strong that I broke my celibacy walk so that he could be fully satisfied. This was the second time in 8 years I had broken my celibacy walk, so I was pretty sure he was the one that would be my future husband. He complained very often about that area being the one thing he really needed in our relationship that he felt was missing. I felt like I could trust him to love me and I knew there were no other women he was dating. I remembered him telling me how I sounded like the wife he had been praying for and how he felt as if he had known me forever. I prayed for him daily, my heart was cracked open, and all I wanted was for him to be as happy and satisfied as I was. So, despite knowing I would be disappointing and disobeying God, I had sex with him.

After that, my heart was fully open. I was sure that I loved him. I felt like he loved me even though he didn't say it directly to me. He would make indirect statements such as, "I wouldn't be with anyone more than a month if I didn't love them." He would look deep into my eyes quite frequently and tell me he wasn't going anywhere; he was staying in my life. He did anything I asked of him, and our bond grew stronger, or so I thought. We continued to spend lots of time together, and I felt like I was finally in a mature and loving relationship.

For this reason, I chose to rationalize, ignore and make excuses for the red flags. Premarital sex has a way of completely clouding your judgement. I prayed more frequently and intensely for him as lifestyle issues that conflicted with my foundational belief system were being exposed. The more I prayed for him, the more my heart opened. The more my heart opened, the softer I felt towards him, even after he began becoming distant. I asked him why he was acting funny; he told me because he was so tired. His shift changed at work, and he was still adjusting to the new schedule. He said he just needed time to get back on track. I used to see him 4-5 days a week, and now I only saw him once a week. He used to stay overnight, but now he would drop me off after a date and go straight home. My heart was pulling closer to him, yet he was pulling away from me. I didn't understand it, but I tried to believe him and give him the time he said he needed.

I got to my breaking point when two weeks went by without me seeing him, and the texts and phone calls became more and more sporadic. I assumed there was another woman. He started to back track on all the promises he made in the beginning and became very secretive. For example, at one disagreement early on, he told me he would not go spend time with female friends unless he ran it pass me first and if I didn't agree with them hanging out, he might not go. Now he was saying to me "I am a grown man. I never said I didn't agree with having female friends, you did." On another occasion, he said I could go through his phone whenever I wanted, and it wouldn't be a big deal. I never went through it; I didn't see a need to. However, one day I asked for it when I noticed his behavior had changed and he told me I had trust issues. Reggie's actions were beginning to stir up the old version of me. When I see signs of disloyalty from the man, I am with, and I address my concerns, I need an immediate positive response to assure me their intentions are pure. When the assurance doesn't come, I grow more suspicious. Like most women of God, I also can discern when something isn't right.

Well, my discernment was correct, and he indeed was spending time with another woman, while pulling away from me. One night we had plans, he didn't show up, answer any of my calls or respond to any of my text messages. He told me the next day he was with a friend, but it wasn't anything sexual. Shortly after this incident, we had another disagreement with no clear resolution and trust was broken. Within three days I broke up with him. I gave him a long speech about how I don't think I was the one for him because it was hard for him to spend quality time with me and once he meets the woman for him, it will be easy to make time for her. I was sure he would stop me from leaving. After all, I believed he loved me. I was sure he would tell me I was wrong about the situation or my discernment was off and ask me to be patient with him. I was sure that within two weeks at the most he would come back to me. Nope, again I was wrong. One week later all communication from Reggie ceased. A few weeks after the breakup, he Facetimed me, but I missed the call. I texted and called back but didn't hear anything else. Two months after that, he Facetimed me again. I was at the office that day and watched my phone light up and vibrate on my desk showing his number only. I had deleted his name and picture from my contacts list, but I still recognized his number. As I stared down at my vibrating phone, I knew in my heart I was done and refused to answer it. I had already made the decision weeks ago that I was done being deceived by Satan for the sake of love, and was trying to get back on track with God.

Satan had deceived me on so many levels with The Good Deacon. I was sure he was a man of integrity who knew God with good fruit on his life. When I visited his church, and watched him serving the Lord in his three-piece suit, collecting the offering and praying on his knees, I believed that was the fruit of his spirituality and relationship with Christ. Being in a relationship with him I felt so loved, I thought it was the love of God. He took care of me and was kind. I learned during this season, that both God and time are the true revealers of all things. God loves his daughters so much he will not allow us to be deceived for too long. He does give us clues through our discernment, before the deception becomes blatant red flags. I believe discernment is a gift from God, along with fruit examination against the Word of God.

However, I must also address the fact that not only did Satan deceive me, but I deceived myself. I deceived myself into thinking that although God's best is not a relationship which opposed his written Word in the Bible, maybe it could become his best through prayer and support. I deceived myself into thinking that if I give him my body, God will forgive me and bless the relationship. After all, God kept telling me to keep praying for him and keep loving him throughout the relationship. God had shown me his heart when I first met him. Surely God would understand that I need to show him my love by making sure his physical needs were met. These were all lies I told myself for the sake of receiving what I thought was real love but turned out to be fake love.

SELF-DECEPTION

Self-deception occurs when we know in our hearts that something isn't right, yet we allow our desires to override our knowledge, wisdom and the Word of God, and our corresponding decisions are based on selfish wants. We ignore the leadership of the Holy Spirit, wise counsel from others and go with what we want to do. Yet, even though we know we are in disobedience or not being smart, we try to pray through the situation in hopes that it will all work out in the end, or God will move supernaturally to make things turn out the way we want them to. Self-deception can lead to a form of witchcraft, in that we are trying to control circumstances with our prayers or make the scripture conform to our lifestyle choices, instead of submitting to God. We deceive and convince ourselves (and sometimes others) of a lie; yet pray that God will get on board with our plan. If we do not repent and get back on track with God's plan, not only will the situation turn out badly, but we will reap the harvest of our decisions with consequences that can be life altering and detrimental to our hearts, minds, spirit and most importantly, our relationship with Christ.

GOD'S LOVE IS MORE POWERFUL THAN ANY FORM OF DECEPTION

Although I made poor choices in the relationship, I am so grateful to God for his mercy and kindness. You see God sees our hearts and he knows every action we are going to take before we take them. I am sure God was shaking his head at me when I said, "but God, I am doing this FOR love!" Since I couldn't get beyond my own self-deception, God intervened for my ultimate protection and swiftly put an end to the relationship. I broke up with Reggie, and he completely disappeared. God's love is so great that he doesn't allow you to suffer long and he also doesn't allow Satan to destroy you. You may hurt, but you're not destroyed. You may be alone and feel lonely, but you're not destroyed. You may be backslidden and broken, but you're not destroyed. God will save, cleanse and restore you again and again, and then allow you to clean yourself up and get back on track with him. That is how powerful the true love of God is. The love of God is amazingly patient and merciful to us, at all times.

Chapter 3

THE BLACK ACTIVIST

Matthew 7:15-20 New King James Version (NKJV)

Beware of false prophets, who come to you in sheep's clothing, but inwardly they are ravenous wolves. You will know them by their fruits. Do men gather grapes from thorn bushes or figs from thistles? Even so, every good tree bears good fruit, but a bad tree bears bad fruit. A good tree cannot bear bad fruit, nor can a bad tree bear good fruit. Every tree that does not bear good fruit is cut down and thrown into the fire. Therefore by their fruits, you will know them.

The scriptural basis for recognizing a red flag in friendship, dating, and courtship can be found in the above reference. The fruit of a man's life reveals what is ultimately in his heart. The peace or drama, positive or negative behavior that is in his life is a direct result of his personal choices and decisions...just like in your own life. Once you recognize a red flag, it is up to you to make the proper decision whether to move on from the relationship or work it out and grow together, if it is possible, with the help of the Holy Spirit.

RED FLAGS IGNORED

As I previously stated I was not fully healed from the relationship and deception experienced with Reggie when I moved onto a new relationship with John. I needed time to process and heal, yet I chose to occupy my time with new men. Let me tell you the story of John, The Black Activist, and how I got to the point of speaking with his side chick. While I do not condone any of my actions and I am not proud of the lengths I went through to find the truth; I am a human being. I am an imperfect woman that is subject the same attacks on my singlehood as any other woman of God. I also have weak areas I thought were permanently dealt with and dead but found out they could be revived under the right circumstances and conditions. I share my story from a place of transparency and total honesty in the hopes that you can relate and know that you are not alone and healing is just as possible for you as it was for me.

As the relationship with Reggie ended what I should have done was take some time to get back on track with God and fully heal. I was so hurt and let down I couldn't think straight. I continued to pray and cry out to God. Unfortunately, however, in the interim, I received some poor advice from a close male family member. My mind was also telling me, similar to his advice, to handle this breakup as I used to handle break ups when I was in my twenties. Get with a new man to get over the old man. After all, plenty of men on the website wanted me, and I was going to keep looking for love there. My family member told me to try dating as men do. Date several men to meet several of my needs until I meet the one who meets all of

Chapter 3

my needs. Again, these words spoke to the old Sarita, in her 20s and how she dated men. These were my before-Christ days, and God was not consulted with how to handle men back in my past life.

So, I began to engage with numerous men, all very different from one another. I still had my minimum standards: church going, non-cursing and agreeing with celibacy until marriage. However, dating in this manner was not easy or peaceful for me. They all wanted time from me, and as a single full time working mother, I didn't have much time to give. I turned down dates and rarely answered phone calls or responded to text messages consistently. Then I started to eliminate those men who weren't keeping my interest, weren't as attractive as I needed them to be or who I discovered had much less going on in their career or ministry than they appeared to once we started getting to know each other.

John stood out amongst the others, and I immediately connected with him. He was youthful and fun. I loved his personality; he made me laugh. He had an interesting perspective on black culture and religion that I partially agreed with and found intriguing. He told me about going to North Carolina to make speeches regarding the state of black men and encourage young men to make wise choices. I admired the fact that he had full custody of his daughter and a great relationship with his mother. Plus, the man was fine. He looked much younger than he was, even though he was older than me, to the point where I had to check his ID to verify his age. He gave me lots of attention, and I was enjoying his companionship. He also spoke to the authentic woman on the inside of me which was one thing Reggie never did. John told me often how beautiful I was and how I better not lose another pound of weight. He told me I was sexy (which he defined as a state of mind and how you carry yourself) and fine. He spoke about how he liked that I lived an organized lifestyle and always picked my brain about financial and investment opportunities. He made me feel highly valuable, smart and desired. When I talked to him about problems at work or with my friends, he encouraged me and seemed to really have my back. He wanted to be the man in my life and help me around the house and with my baby. These were all the things my damaged soul was crying out for which he gave freely, and my heart opened up to him.

The first red flag came only a few weeks after talking as friends. He called me one night I didn't answer, then he texted me that he needed to talk. When I called him back later that night, he told me about how he had just left his daughter's mom's house because he was trying to see if she would babysit their two-year-old daughter. When he got there, she was smoking crack with her boyfriend. John lost his temper, broke the pipe, broke her phone, tore up her house, slapped her boyfriend and left. He said the only thing he felt bad about breaking her phone. I got off the phone with him after a few minutes and did not answer anymore of his calls or respond to his text messages for two weeks. I knew that was too much potential drama for me and I wanted no parts of it.

During this two-week period, I continued to talk to the other five men I was engaging. None of those friendships were growing, however, and I was bored with all of them. I decided to call John. I told myself that although he had issues with his daughter's mom, we could still be friends. We might not get into a relationship and what transpires between him and his daughter's mom really wasn't my business. We could just talk on a friendship level, and that would be okay. I would not get close to him.

Chapter 3

That was the worst decision ever. I should have paid attention to that red flag and stayed away. I believe it was God revealing the fruit in this man's life which was the opposite of my own fruitful life. I live a simple life with much peace and joy. John had a lot going on and even by just being friends with him I ran the risk of getting close to him. Then his drama would become my drama because he lives a life of deceit and ungodliness, as I later found out. That was a huge warning sign that scared me away, but not enough to prevent me from reopening the door and allowing him back into my life.

The more we spent time together, the closer we became. So, close that I broke my celibacy walk…again. The 3rd fall in 8 years of my celibacy journey. I rationalized as I did with Reggie, that I was doing it for the sake of being loved and him potentially becoming my husband. As I let him into my intimate space, I began to ignore other red flags and discernment from God that his heart wasn't pure and he was not a true man of God. Once my body parts were given, my heart was also open. The sex was pretty good, and that clouded my judgement even more. I saw him through rose colored lenses, ignored heaven's warnings and when he began telling me he loved me, I believed him each time. I asked myself, do I really love him? I never said it back because I was unsure. After a few months, I gave in. I allowed my heart to open and told him I loved him too. We decided to be in a relationship from that point forward, and I was happy being with him.

I thought that we were equally yoked since he said he believed Jesus was his Lord and Savior. He told me how he grew up in church and prayed every day. When we talked about spiritual matters, he would say how important it was to not only teach our children about God but also about where Christianity started and how it has affected the black community. He led me to believe he was passionate about teaching children and black youth to believe in themselves and realize they were kings and queens. He told me about a recent trip to North Carolina where he spoke at his uncle's church giving a message to encourage the youth in that city. He sent me messages and videos about how strong and valuable black women were and how black men must step up and take care of women since nations are birthed from us. I was intrigued by his beliefs and agreed with most of his points. However, when I asked him if he heard from God during prayer, his response made me question his relationship with Christ. He heard from God based on how circumstances would change after he prayed, but he never heard his voice. I knew I wanted a man of God who could hear the voice of God as I do when I pray and as the Bible teaches. So, I continued to pray that he would not only seek God in prayer, but begin to hear the Lord's still small voice.

Other issues started to arise in our relationship as time went on. I noticed that John always took his cell phone everywhere he went, he never left it alone around me. He even took it with him in the shower. That was major red flag that he had a convincing argument for that was rooted in me having trust issues. He told me he did not have a Facebook account, yet I discovered an account under a made-up name a few weeks after that. He never let me come inside his house. This was okay at first because I wanted to be in my own home with my son and all his baby stuff. As time went on, however, I wanted to go and see his home and how he was living. Although he said, I could come whenever I wanted to, when I would ask to come visit there was always an excuse why I could not come. He also would not answer his phone and respond sporadically to text when he was with his family. When I questioned those things, he accused me time and time again of having jealousy and trust issues. He told me I was pushing him away whenever I asked him about these things that were raising red flags.

***

TRUST YOURSELF

I do not believe that when a woman notices some things that aren't quite right following her intuition and she begins to question those things that she is the one with trust issues. We are smart and intelligent women who know what love, honesty, and faithfulness look like. We know how it feels. It is peaceful. The responses from your man when questioning his behavior should also lead to peace, comfort, and love. When a man is forthright and honest, and his woman is truly tripping for no reason, he can bring her encouragement, compassion, and security. There is nothing wrong with a man making his woman feel secure. Especially when he is in a relationship with a woman over 30 years old. Most of us in this age group have been through and experienced a lot in life. Sometimes we may need assurance that this isn't the same pattern in a new man that will lead to heartache and wasted time. While I do understand that everyone is different and there are most certainly exceptions, most of the time, we can trust ourselves and the discernment given by God.

***

For about two weeks before I got confirmation that my discernment was correct, John began becoming very distant. He said it was because he was feeling depressed and stressed due to issues with his daughter's mom and because his car broke down. When he did not answer some of my calls, he would tell me it was because he just needed time to himself. When he did not allow me to come around, he told me he just needed to be with his daughter since that brings him so much joy. Sometimes he would say he was with his mom, or at church, or with his grandmother. I tried to encourage him and be understanding. I sent him short sermons, quotes about strength in God and prayer, and I even wrote him a few poems about how I saw him as a King and expressing my love for him. I did my best to be patient and decided to trust him and stop questioning him about whether there was another woman and simply be supportive during his rough season. I was not at all prepared for what would happen next.

Chapter 4

THE REBIRTH OF THE CRAZY GIRL

Romans 7:15-20 Amplified Bible (AMP)

For I do not understand my own actions [I am baffled and bewildered by them]. I do not practice what I want to do, but I am doing the very thing I hate [and yielding to my human nature, my worldliness—my sinful capacity]. Now if I habitually do what I do not want to do, [that means], I agree with the Law, confessing that it is good (morally excellent). So now [if that is the case, then] it is no longer I who do it [the disobedient thing which I despise], but the sin [nature] which lives in me. For I know that nothing good lives in me, that is, in my flesh [my human nature, my worldliness—my sinful capacity]. For the willingness [to do good] is present in me, but the doing of good is not. For the good that I want to do, I do not do, but I practice the very evil that I do not want. But if I am doing the very thing I do not want to do; I am no longer the one doing it [that is, it is not me that acts], but the sin [nature] which lives in me.

How to Heal a Broken Heart

None of us are perfect. Paul was an amazing apostle of God and yet still struggled with his sinful nature. We strive to be more Christ-like each and every day. However, we all have our weak areas and moments. Even though you have weak moments or may end up backslidden, by the grace of God you can get back on track in your holiness walk. As you are open and honest with God in your prayer time, his grace and strength will flow through your heart, and your decisions and actions will begin to line up with his will for your life once again.

DON'T FEED THE MONSTER

During the two weeks that John started becoming distant, my mind was racing and constantly playing the guessing game. I was stressed and hurting because I didn't understand why he wouldn't let me be there for him. I knew something wasn't right. My mind reflected back on past relationships of heartbreak and men who lied and had other women on the side. I became very anxious when I couldn't get a clear answer from him. I started to self-medicate using old methods I had been delivered from for nine years. I was smoking and drinking. I felt like those things would calm my spirit and take my mind off of him. They only made matters worse.

He continued to come around, but much less than before. He insisted that there was no other woman and that I had trust issues. He persisted with the fact that he just needed to get himself together but that he loved me and absolutely needed me in his life. He said he did not want to lose me forever and asked me to just be patient with him during this time.

Meanwhile, I was feeding the monster AKA the Crazy Girl, which was what I called my carnal, sinful nature. I fed the monster not only through self-medication but also by looking through all this social media profiles, since he posted his every move throughout the day, and listening to music that spoke to my pain and rage while igniting vengeful thoughts of being "savage" towards men. The Crazy Girl that I thought was dead was reborn. The alcohol only exasperated my feelings. Late at night, I would dig for the truth using several investigative methods. I obtained reports confirming his addresses, felony convictions, family members names, where he grew up at, etc. I believe the reason I spiraled so quickly into this backslidden condition, of smoking, drinking, cursing, snooping and becoming vengeful, was because I was not fully healed and whole from the failed relationship with Reggie. I needed time to process the poor choices I made back then, but instead, I jumped right into a relationship with John. My heart was in a damaged state going into the situation, so his behavior brought out the worst side of me expeditiously and in a greater measure than what I experienced when Reggie broke my heart. Although I was not being led by the Spirit of God but by my flesh, I still prayed. I asked God to reveal his heart, character and true intentions. I asked God to let all things be revealed.

THE MONSTER BIRTHS THE CRAZY GIRL

The next night after I fed the monster, I allowed the Crazy Girl to do what she does. I contacted two women on his Facebook, his daughter's mom and who I assumed was the girl he was cheating on me with. I knew one of them had to be the real reason he was lying and hiding things from me.

TRANSPARENCY IN LOVE

As I have stated before I do not condone any of my actions. However, I am completely transparent with my story in hopes of helping you not make the same mistakes I made and if you have, helping you to heal and move on from past heartbreak. I do not believe in projecting a perfect image even though I strive to be Christ-like every single day. This walk of singleness is not always easy, especially as we grow older and the years seem to fly by. We have all done things we are not proud of. As ashamed or embarrassed as I could be about my actions, I believe that hiding has no benefit. I have chosen to use what Satan meant for evil and give God the glory, by sharing my honest accounts of mistakes made and lesson learned. I encourage you to do the same in your own situation. Once you have grown, healed and learned valuable lessons used to transform your life, share your story with others in your own way. Allow your testimony to birth hope and healing in others.

John was clearly not the man for me. I realized this hard truth over the two weeks of turmoil. I could tell by examining his communication, patterns and red flags which I was unable to ignore any longer. This relationship was triggering my anxiety and provoking my "crazy side". The man for you will add value and encourage you towards God and purpose, not provoke you in the opposite direction. He will not influence you in a way that would lead you back to the person you were delivered from. He will not help to feed your monster or ignite old negative behaviors, even if indirectly.

Even if it were true that John needed space and time to deal with personal issues, he would have made me feel secure in the relationship. His communication would have been mature, and he would have led our relationship to a peaceful place. Instead of hiding, he would have been transparent. Yet, transparency was impossible because he was indeed being unfaithful. I asked God to reveal all things that I could not see. I should have prayed to God sooner to reveal his true intentions to me, but I thought I could see them through his actions. At this point, time was revealing his character, and God answered my prayer swiftly.

ALL THINGS ARE REVEALED

I will reiterate, am not proud of my actions, but they did lead me to the truth. I could still be in a fake relationship with John if I had not prayed and sought out the truth. I believe it was God that led me to the truth, even as the Crazy Girl investigated. Of all the women on his Facebook page with the fake profile name, I knew exactly who to contact…and I was right.

I sent her one message asking her if she was messing with my man. She didn't respond. However, John put a post on his page about missing her. Of course, that night he wasn't answering my phone calls again. The rage inside of me was like fire when I saw his post, and as I fed the monster with self-medication, I needed more information. I knew exactly how to get it. I sent her a second message to provoke her into a response and gain answers. My plan worked. Immediately she responded, "He is right here. If you have something to say, here is my number."

My stomach dropped. I couldn't dial her number fast enough. I knew the relationship between me and him was over, but the Crazy Girl needed answers. I knew his side chick was pregnant because of posts on her page showing her swelling belly and ultrasound pictures. I needed to know if it was his baby, how long they had been together, and if I was actually the side chick this whole time. He had previously told me that this woman was his daughter's aunt when he mistakenly called me by her name one day, and I asked him who she was. This was during the period that he claimed he was depressed and needed time to himself. On another occasion, he told me that she was an old friend when I saw him post on his page and tag her in it. When I called her this night, I was finally going to get the truth.

She told me they had only been together for a few weeks and that they had met on Facebook. When she asked him about my first message and who I was, he had told her that we only had a one-night encounter and he didn't talk to me anymore. He also told her I was crazy and not to listen to me. I told her that we had been together for a while and he was just at my house less than two weeks prior and we spoke on the phone every day. I told her how he told me that she was just his daughter's aunt, and that he loved me. She said that their relationship was definitely over and that she believed what I was telling her about me and him. All while he was in the background begging her to listen to him. My heart was breaking more and more with each moment of this 10-minute phone call. I didn't understand how the man who said he loved me, the man I decided to fully trust was begging her and acting as if I was no one in his life. He called me from another room while I was on the phone with her, saying that I was too jealous. I hung up on him and got more information from his side chick. Since they had met on Facebook just a few weeks prior, that wasn't his baby. She asked for screenshots to prove that I was telling her the truth. I sent her a few of him telling me he loved me. He claimed I broke into his Instagram account and sent those messages to myself. I couldn't send screenshots of text messages he had sent directly to my phone because I deleted our conversations and his number from my phonebook a few days prior since I knew something wasn't right and I needed to end the relationship. I planned to simply erase him out of my life, but only after I got the answers I needed.

THE CONSEQUENCE OF IGNORING RED FLAGS

As I stated before, had I listened to the red flags early on, I would not have gotten to this point. His drama had truly become my drama. His issues became my issues. He loved me with a fake love, but I gave him real love. His love hurt while my love encouraged. No man should ever cause the woman he loves to think that she is the one with the problem, has jealousy or trust issues while he is being untrue and manipulative.

When I hung up the phone, I literally was in shock. I couldn't believe that he was placing this woman's feelings before mine. I couldn't believe that our history didn't mean anything to him, but rather this new situation with her was his priority. It cut me to the core to hear him beg her and toss me to side. I waited for my phone to ring all night. I just knew he would call me to make things right. I didn't sleep a wink but instead self-medicated and took sleeping pills so I could get up for work in the morning. My anxiety was screaming, and I didn't sleep more than 10 minutes at a time. My peace was completely gone.

The call from John did not come that sleepless night, but it came the next day. I went into the office for only one hour and had to leave early since my mind was racing and there was no way I could focus on work. I didn't answer his first 16 calls, I only responded with texts. By then, the Crazy Girl was in full blown crazy-mode. I called him every demeaning name I could. I cursed and yelled. I wished curses on his life and threatened to have my boys shoot his lips off. I told him he was Satan and never to call me again.

When I finally answered the phone that afternoon, I was an emotional wreck. He could tell I was crying and offered words to try and calm me down. Within five minutes the Crazy Girl was attacking him again with yelling and cursing. He said he knew he deserved every word I threw at him, but that he didn't mean to hurt me and he wasn't trying to break my heart. He told me he loved me. He wanted to see me that day. I told him I never wanted to see him again. We hung up that afternoon, and I continued feeding the monster at a much higher consumption rate to numb the pain.

My spirit was being tormented with guilt for breaking my celibacy walk, anger, and anxiety towards John. I did continue to pray in the midst of it all. But instead of getting into the Word and on my face before the Lord, I went back to the liquor bottle. I answered the rest of his calls that same evening. He told me how he didn't know he meant that much to me or that I would care so much that he cheated. He told me that he didn't think he deserved me. He said that he still loved me and wanted to be with me. He even invited me on a trip out of town that upcoming weekend. When he said that he would call me back and then didn't answer the phone the rest of the night, I knew he was still with his new woman despite those manipulative conversations we had throughout the day. I blocked him that night so that he could not reach me again. It was time for me to start the healing process, let him go and move on with my life.

PART 2

The Journey to Peace and Healing

BREAKTHROUGH, DELIVERANCE, AND FREEDOM

Chapter 5

THE DEATH OF THE CRAZY GIRL

Romans 8:13 Amplified Bible (AMP)

For if you are living according to the [impulses of the] flesh, you are going to die. But if [you are living] by the [power of the Holy] Spirit you are habitually putting to death the sinful deeds of the body, you will [really] live forever.

God's desire is for your life to bring him glory so that you can be a blessing to others and also lead others to Christ. If your lifestyle opposes his will and his Word, he cannot move in your life the way he would like to with blessing and power. Your fleshly desires and sinful nature must die so that Christ can live through you and others can witness the Lord's goodness. You must starve your flesh by removing and abstaining from those things that feed your sinful nature and feed your spirit by filling your mind, heart, and space with the Word of God, worship, and prayer.

STARVE THE MONSTER, FEED THE SPIRIT

Although I blocked John's number, I continued to feed the monster. I fed the monster not only with alcohol and cigarettes but also by looking on his Facebook page, downloading a full background report and checking his new woman's page to see what they were up to. Two days after I blocked him, I unblocked him, and we had a long conversation. It was a friendly conversation although I did throw jabs and shade about his new, and pregnant, girlfriend which he was still denying. All of this behavior was still feeding the monster which was not what I needed. I couldn't heal, I couldn't focus on anything else, and I couldn't move on. I knew that I needed to starve the monster, kill the Crazy Girl and heal through the power and love of God. I knew that only through Christ could I get my sanity back, control my thoughts and emotions and truly heal. I also knew I wanted to heal quickly because I didn't want to stay in this condition. I needed to be whole, focused and happy to be the best mom and Christian woman I could be.

I immediately called a spiritual fast. Normally I would put my baby to sleep then either talk on the phone with John or watch my favorite TV shows. Now, I was going to go deep into God and get my healing speedily and permanently. I pulled out a book a bought almost two years prior, called The Bait of Satan by John Bevere. The book is about healing from offense, past hurts, and pains. Although the focus was on church hurt, the words ministered to my spirit and were perfect for my current situation. As I read through the pages, I could clearly see how Satan was using John to steal my joy, kill my peace and destroy my faith that God would send me a good loving man. Satan wanted me to believe that the love we shared was the best love ever. Satan is the father of lies. He wanted me to believe that maybe there is hope, when John gets his act together, so I should just stick with him and not give up. He also wanted me to believe that self-medicating felt good. That it numbed the pain. That it would be okay to have just one more conversation with John. He wanted me to believe that maybe it was something I did to cause the relationship to go south. That perhaps if I had said the right thing on this particular day before he started cheating, he would have never cheated. Maybe if I wouldn't have asked him for too much, John would still be with me. Satan wanted me to believe that I do have trust issues and no man will ever stick around for the long term with me. These were all lies. I could clearly see they were lies the more I read, the more I said the declarations from the book out loud and the more I prayed to God.

HOLY SPIRIT LED WRITING FOR BREAKTHROUGH

One day I was reading on my lunch break and was inspired to write out my feelings. I am a writer, so most times God helps me to process negative and positive emotions by writing. I needed to write and see the words in the front of me. I tore out a piece of legal pad paper from a notepad nearby and wrote: "The Monster AKA the Crazy Girl" on one side. Then I listed all the behaviors and attributes that I wanted to die immediately.

- Smoking, cursing, drinking
- Lust, craving and desiring John's body and sex
- Offense and hurt from all the men in my past
- Desire and love for John
- Bitterness towards men and John
- Hate towards John and myself
- Sadness about being single and mistreated

- Envy of other women who had the blessed marriages I desired for myself

- Uncontrollable thoughts and behavior

- Anxiety, fear, jealousy

Can you relate to anything on this list? You see I started to hate John for breaking my heart and not trying to provide an immediate remedy. He was trying to keep me and this other woman in a relationship with him at the same time even after he got caught. I hated him for not loving me like he claimed to. I hated myself for not listening to the red flags and following my discernment early on. I hated myself for breaking my celibacy walk again and placing a man's love above God. I started to replay all the hurts of men in my past and started becoming more and more depressed about the cycle I lived in. Most of the men that broke my heart have since went on to get married and appear to be happy. That fact seemed unfair and unjust. The bitterness towards them was taking over my thoughts. Some of the items on the list I didn't even realize were taking place within my heart. God was the one who revealed to me that I was envious of a certain coworker. I was asking God this same day why hearing her voice was so annoying. The Lord said to me it's because you are envious. She has what you want. She has the husband, the children, the career, and she always looks cute. She seemingly has it all. I was shocked in that moment. I didn't even know I had envy in my heart. Yet, as I was completely transparent and honest with myself and God, he revealed even more areas of a needed breakthrough which I added to the list. The Lord did this because he also wanted the monster to die and me to heal so that I could move forward with his purpose for my life.

Chapter 5

I flipped the page over and wrote down words of life. I wrote who I knew I was as a woman of God, despite my present spiritual, mental and emotional state. This side of the paper was titled: Sarita.

- Loving, caring, peaceful, joyful
- I am like God
- I live like God
- God has control of my mind and body
- I think like God
- I forgive like God
- I make wise decisions
- I live according to the Word and words of God (that I hear in prayer)
- I live according to the desires of God
- I sow seeds of goodness, peace, love, understanding, and patience
- I am led ONLY by the Spirit of God
- My thoughts and ways are God's thoughts and ways
- I hear from God daily and immediately obey his wisdom, leadership, and discernment
- I am a woman of great faith
- I believe in the power and love of God

This is the woman I truly am. Not the Crazy Girl. I decided not to identify myself with the monster anymore. Instead of saying the monster was a part of me, I separated the real me which was my renewed spirit through Christ, from the carnal nature of my flesh. We are spirit beings. Through salvation, we have eternal life. Our spirits will join our Heavenly Father once this flesh is returned to dust. This flesh, is not the real me. My spirit filled with the Holy Spirit that is the real me. This is the person that God sees. Once we receive salvation, he doesn't see our sin. God sees our renewed spirits, made one with him. He sees us blameless. This is because he sees our spirits, he sees our hearts. God is not caught up on punishing us or condemning us for the mistakes our flesh makes. He has abundant grace, mercy and loving kindness for those moments in time.

For this reason, God still blessed me, protected me and spoke to me even as the Crazy Girl was acting a straight up fool. His grace was sufficient for that moment. He knew that I would get back on track with him through authentic repentance. He knew that for the sake of love, I had compromised my standards and made a man my idol. My Father understood that I would begin making ungodly decisions even before I made them. Yet he had a plan to keep me close to him, heal my broken heart and kill the monster the entire time. There is truly nothing like the love of God.

Chapter 6

THE PEACE PROCESS

Colossians 3:2-3 Amplified Bible (AMP)

Set your mind and keep focused habitually on the things above [the heavenly things], not on things that are on the earth [which have only temporal value]. For you died [to this world], and your [new, real] life is hidden with Christ in God.

As you set your mind on heavenly things, that is living your life the way God wants you to live, focusing on those things that bring him the most glory and placing priority on calling and purpose, you will experience great peace. God does not want you depressed, hurting, bitter or constantly living in frustration. Make your life peaceful. Organize your life in a way that flows with God and produces much peace and joy and helps you keep your mind set on things above.

GETTING MY PEACE BACK

There was a process of healing my broken heart. I knew I couldn't go through the process alone. I spoke to a man of God who happened to also be a Relationship Coach. I had previously talked to him about Reggie, and he told me if I ever needed to talk to him again, he would be there for me. So when I found out about John's cheating, I confided in him for encouragement and to get a male's perspective on the situation. He gave me the best advice. He told me that John was not a good man of God by the simple fact that he was cheating on me and also playing games with a pregnant girl. That spoke volumes of his lack of character and integrity. He told me what I already knew, that I needed to remove myself from the situation. His advice was to block him on the phone and all social media. He told me not to talk to him anymore because that will only make things worse. He also encouraged me to see the blessing in the situation. I told him I didn't feel blessed. I was hurting. My heart was broken. How could I be blessed? He told me that even though these things were revealed now, at least John's true character came out after months of being in a relationship with him instead of years later. He showed me that even though my heart was tied up in John, we didn't have anything physically tying us together. Our lives were not entangled. I could easily walk away. We had no children together, no home together, no finances or bills intertwined. All I had to do was remove myself, disconnect all communications and move on with my life. He also encouraged me to share my story with other women. He knew I was a writer and told me to write about it. I told him I was ashamed and embarrassed; I didn't want to share this struggle. On the contrary, I wanted to hide. I felt like a hypocrite. How can I encourage and empower single women when I myself had made so many mistakes concerning these last two relationships? However, he reminded me that I too am human. I make mistakes just like everyone else. I too have struggled. I am not perfect. Jesus was the only perfect human to walk the earth. Sharing my story through writing would absolutely help other women.

A WORD OF ENCOURAGEMENT

Although this example of heartbreak ended prior to marriage, children or years invested, there is still much hope if you are in one these situations. I also have a son from a relationship which ended in heartbreak which I will describe in greater detail momentarily. The key is to focus on God's promise of restoration. God will restore the years, time and energy invested into a relationship that comes to an end. You are still a blessed woman because it did not permanently knock you down or take you out. You can and will get back up again, heal and may even enter into a new God-ordained relationship with a man that is heaven sent for you. You have not lost all hope, as you shouldn't; therefore, God's promises are still available for you. Also, if you have ties to someone who broke your heart, you have an opportunity to turn what the enemy meant for evil and give God the glory from it. Remember, all things are working together for your good. Get the wisdom of God for the situation to determine how to move forward in a manner that will bring him the most glory. Access his grace and strength to help you move forward with your life into a place of peace that surpasses all understanding.

This man of God's words to me at my lowest moment was wisdom from God. It reminded me of some advice I had gotten years ago when my heart was broken by the hands of another man. In this situation, I was with this man for almost two years. Then one day, out of nowhere he told me he had gotten married the night before. I was shocked, and my heart was torn into pieces. How could he have gotten married when we were in a relationship for almost two years? I sought out encouragement from another man of God with much fruit on his life this time as well. He told me the exact same thing, to see the blessing in it. Again, I told him, I feel cursed not blessed. How am I blessed, my heart is completely broken? He said, well Sarita, would you rather that have been you? Would you rather he married you and been cheating on you the whole time? As a matter of fact, he will still cheat on her because he hasn't changed. There was no repentance on his behalf with God. He cheated on her the whole time and then married her. Would you rather be married to a man who is a cheater? That is the blessing. You are free to move on with your life. She is now married to someone who doesn't know what true love is and has no integrity as a man.

Both of these men of God were right. I was free. I could move on with my life. The memories will remain and moments of hurt may appear, but I have no ties to the men who had no regard for my heart. The new women they are with will soon experience heart ache by these men simply because they have un-repented hearts and are not remorseful for their actions. The fact that they have women on top of women shows they have not changed. No time had passed for them to change or grow. Just because they appear to now have chosen the woman they want to be with, they are still the same men who lied and cheated. They are still the same men who hid actions and behaviors that they knew were not right which would cause hurt and pain, yet chose to continue in their ways. John didn't come clean and turn his life around. He got caught. Then he continued to lie. His new relationship is built on lies. God's blessing is not in lies and manipulation. God's blessing is in integrity, love, and peace.

Chapter 6

The people we turn to during times of hurt can help our healing process or slow it down. These must be people of God who have fruit on their lives that godly living will produce. These individuals do not have to be perfect, but they should exhibit the qualities of God. During both these instances, the words of these men of God were inspired by the Holy Spirit. I left both conversations feeling encouraged and truly protected by my Heavenly Father. The Lord answered my prayers to reveal their character and swiftly removed both men from my life who did not truly love me as they professed to. Not only did I feel better, after consulting these men of God, but I was empowered to help others, fulfilling my godly purpose through ministry. I didn't feel worse about myself, condemned by my poor decisions or silly for believing and trusting them. I only felt blessed and motivated to grow closer to God.

GETTING BACK TO "ME"

The next step I took to get my peace back was to remember where I was before John and even before Reggie entered my life. I had to fill my days with personal goals and fun activities. I was loving on my baby, settling into a new home I purchased that same year and meeting my financial and spiritual goals. I had lost 50 pounds of the baby weight that I gained. I worked on encouraging women through the Phenomenal Single Woman coaching practice, with books, blogs, Instagram posts, downloadable resources, and programs. I was in the Word daily gaining great insight into singleness and preparing to launch programs for women 30 years old and above. Just for fun, I was creating baby care advice videos, taking beach trips and enjoying finding new creative toddler activities.

To encourage myself I wrote down a brand new list of what the next man must possess, in order, for me to be in a relationship with him. I had previously discarded my list because I didn't want to limit God or be too picky. At that time, I only prayed for a man who was filled with and led by the Holy Spirit of God. I left the other details up to the Lord because he knows the desires of my heart. I realized that I needed a written list, because I am a writer who functions best with words in front of me. The list is not for God's sake, but for my own faith walk. It would remind me of what I ultimately need and deserve in my man, even if the relationship does not lead to marriage. It also will help me to stay focused and not become distracted by counterfeits. I posted this list to the front of my refrigerator.

These are practical ways in which I keep my mind on the things above so I can maintain peace. I know that God created me to teach and encourage. He also created me to be a beauty girl. I love all things hair, makeup, and nails. I am as prissy and girly as they come. I focus on the woman God created me to be by doing the things he placed inside of me for myself, my baby, women of God and in market place ministry at my job. I focus on Christ by being the woman Christ created me to be and embracing my authenticity and creativity. I also began to write about this very trying season, which is the birth of this book.

SHIFTING FOCUS AND GETTING WHOLE AGAIN

I also wrote down my immediate goals to get back to peace. I wrote down the things that I have to look forward to each day that brings me joy. In the morning, I look forward to my delicious chocolate coffee and putting on a beautiful full face of makeup for the day while I listen to worship music in the background. Those moments to myself in the early morning give me such joy and peace. While at work I would look forward to teaching and training through my daily task and interactions with staff. I love helping others, and I needed to focus on marketplace ministry, not just going through the motions of working. In the evening I look forward to spending time with my son, teaching him and learning about his milestones and developmental growth. I enjoy preparing his meals and watching him grow into a little man. On the weekends I look forward to creating new and fun things for us to do together and things for me to do for myself. I planned out our trips and getaways and encouraged myself by reminding myself of the vision and plans God has for me.

Lastly, I worked on getting whole in my spirit and heart in order to get back to my place of peace. I watched a powerful teaching called Sexual Wholeness by Pastor Toure Roberts. I knew that since all the past hurts from prior relationships was resurfacing; I needed to break the current soul tie with John and all the others that lingered unbeknownst to me. I was in tears as I watched and listened to this compelling message of the true intentional of godly sexual relationships between a husband and wife and the spiritual, mental and emotional consequences of premarital sex. I received every word of wisdom and the powerful closing prayer of deliverance. In that moment I sensed the burden removing, yoke destroying power of God come upon me, right there behind the closed door of my office in front of my computer screen. I was on my lunch break, and I could hardly contain my whispered yet intense praise and worship so as not to disturb my coworkers. I was truly free from my past, and the soul ties held me no longer. I felt immediately liberated. My heart was no longer attached to John; my body no longer craved his. The desire I had for him to be close even while I was hurting was completely gone. I believe I truly had a supernatural encounter with God and immediate deliverance from soul ties and emotional bondage.

I wanted to get back on my celibacy walk with God as I started this new season of renewed peace. There was no peace within myself fornicating. It seemed peaceful, but during the aftermath, I felt tormented. Your spirit is wrestling with your flesh, yet your desire is to please God. You feel weak, and you become entangled. Then comes the guilt and condemnation and you rationalize with God that you are doing it for the sake of love. I needed to end this cycle immediately. My heart and spirit were so open to receive this breakthrough; I believe that is why it manifested so quickly and thoroughly.

Chapter 7

NEVER STOP PRAYING

---

1 Thessalonians 5:16-18 Amplified Bible (AMP)

Rejoice always and delight in your faith; be unceasing and persistent in prayer; in every situation [no matter what the circumstances] be thankful and continually give thanks to God; for this is the will of God for you in Christ Jesus.

I heard a preacher once say when he told someone to go and pray about their situation, the person dropped their head and asked rhetorically, "That's all you want me to do, just pray?" He was shocked by their response and knew they didn't have a full revelation of the power of prayer. His response to them was "What do you mean, 'just pray'? Praying the most powerful thing you can do!" I agree with this preacher. Our prayers do not hit the ceiling if they are heart felt and based on the Word of God. Prayer is extremely powerful and is the only thing that can change even the most seemingly impossible situations.

PRAY THROUGH THE PAIN

Sometimes when our heart is broken, we do not feel like praying. Especially if we broke any promise, we made to God including our celibacy walk with Him. We feel guilty. We feel cut to the core. We feel stupid. Perhaps we do pray and can't hear God speaking to our hearts, so we think, what's the point? We know that eventually, we will start praying again, but we just can't seem to bring ourselves into His presence right now. The guilt, shame, and humiliation are an invisible barrier between us and the throne of God.

As I shared earlier, even in the mist of my sin with John I prayed. Even when the monster was in full blown crazy mode, I prayed. I couldn't hear from God. The thoughts of hatred and revenge were so loud…yet I still prayed. I learned from another past failed relationship to always keep praying no matter what, pray through the pain.

A few years ago, I was very active in my local church, and I started dating an usher. I just knew this was God's will because an elder of the church looked at us both one day and said: "You two would make such a cute couple." We had already been chatting and flirting here and there, but I was hesitant to give him my number. He didn't meet my standards as far as where he was in life professionally and financially, although he appeared to meet my spiritual and physical standards. To make a long story short, we got together, and a few weeks into the relationship I discovered that he still was hanging out with another girl at the church. He had very strong feelings for her, and I had no idea they were that close. At the end of our brief relationship, he left me to be with her. I was all alone, and they were together for a few years after that. It was extremely painful to see them at church and events 3-4 times per week, in the church parking lot or sitting together in the row directly in front of me. I was hurt because I really wanted the relationship to work out and I truly believed God was leading us to be together.

As this relationship ended, I felt like I couldn't pray. I did not want to pray. I was hurt, but instead of running into the arms of my Heavenly Father I felt a barrier between us. I had not broken my celibacy walk with the usher, but we got very close on a few occasions. I was ashamed of those moments and allowing myself to get so close to him too quickly. I felt like I needed to hide what I was going through from God. I could sing worship songs and lift my hands in his presence. Yet, I could not bring myself to pray.

I spoke to a good friend of mine at the time, and she encouraged me not only to pray but to be fully transparent with God. She reminded me that God sees what's in our hearts, he is right there with us in those shameful moments and he still loves us. Why not bare all in prayer? That's the best way to receive his love, strength, and encouragement. No one can strengthen you or encourage you like your Creator. He loves us so very much. He chose us to be his children. We are hand selected by the Almighty Father to belong to him. We are so special to Him. As my friend told me, he knows everything anyway, so why not open our hearts and communicate wholly in prayer.

CONTINUAL TRANSPARENT PRAYER

I believe the reason I received such expeditious healing after the breakup with John is because of my prayer life. I have a very real, very transparent prayer life with God. I talk to him about everything, even the darkest things. I do this because I want his help with everything without limitation. I had found that when I hid things during my prayer time because I was so ashamed or guilty, I would struggle for much longer in the area

I needed to grow in. Sometimes I never received breakthrough at all until I could verbalize it honestly and directly to God.

YOUR HEAVENLY PRAYER LANGUAGE

As I mentioned earlier, I pray in both English and in my heavenly prayer language always. I understand this is a controversial subject and I will not go into great depth, but will explain as simply as possible. If you have received the baptism of the Holy Spirit with the evidence of prayer tongues, I encourage you to pray in English and in tongues continually. If you have not received the gift, simply ask God for it. It will manifest for you if you believe, you are able to receive this gift of power by faith. The Bible teaches about 3 types of tongues; I am only speaking about prayer tongues (not tongues that need interpretation and not another known language), which is your heavenly prayer language. There are many scriptures to study regarding this gift, but I will highlight Acts 19:1-7 which is the easiest to follow example I know of how to receive this gift, although it is not necessary to have an apostle lay hands on you. I myself received the gift by faith alone in my prayer closet one evening. While I do believe praying in tongues allows access to an amazing endowment of edification and power, I do not believe prayer tongues is a requirement for healing, breakthrough or deliverance. I do believe it is a gift of supernatural power (Acts 1:8) to help you permanently and quickly overcome any obstacle and hear from God directly with great clarity in times of need.

Here is a final example of the importance of continual transparent prayer even while in sin and/or healing from a broken heart. When I got pregnant with my son, I was at the lowest point ever in my spiritual journey. I had been celibate

Chapter 7

for 6 years straight at this point, yet I lowered my standards and compromised my body for my best friend, Jason. I had known him since high school for 17 years. I thought he was nice, compassionate and light hearted. We used to have so much fun together, hanging out, reminiscing and talking about almost everything. What I didn't realize was that our relationship was very surface level, which is why it was so light and fun, we never had an argument of any kind. We never had any in depth conversations about relationships, culture or spirituality. We had become distant friends over the years, but I decided to give us a chance to become closer. You notice I said that I decided... not God. After all, he was my best male friend, and everyone always says, you should marry your best friend. We had talked about the possibility of a relationship a few times, but I was always hesitant and never wanted to move forward. I noticed some red flags and even some relationship deal breakers, but thought maybe he just needed a good woman to help him become the best man I knew he could be. I saw great potential in him, and I trusted him. Everything started off cool, we traveled, hung out with friends and family and supported each other's business ideas. However, things would rather quickly take a turn for the worst.

All the optimism and hope I had at the onset of our dating relationship was quickly destroyed as reality set in. I saw a side of him that I did not know existed as we got closer and real-life issues were exposed. Our whirlwind relationship was full of drama, fighting, and tears. It was verbally and emotionally abusive. As time went on, I could see signs that it would become physically abusive as well if I would have stayed with him. All the warning signs were there. I broke up with him less than a month after I found out I was pregnant.

The decision to end things with Jason was completely led by God. Even in the mist of fornication and disobedience I never stopped praying, and I was still going to church and serving in ministry. This was one of the most difficult decisions I have ever made. Through the hurt and trauma, the relationship caused on my soul, I still had a love for Jason and cared about his feelings. I did not want to hurt him, and I wanted to make the best decision for our unborn child. Right before I broke up with him, I prayed wholeheartedly for direction from God. After all, who breaks up with the father of their child when they are still in a relationship with him? Most women would try to work things out. As a matter of fact, I did get advice from some girlfriends to see if I could work it out. However, they did not know the depth of the drama which took place behind closed doors. So their advice was well intentioned, but they did not have the full story. I am still not sure when or if I will ever share all the details of what transpired between us.

The night I asked God for clear direction he gave me a dream that helped me make my decision. In the dream, I was driving up a mountain on a four-lane highway. All the lanes were going in the same direction. I was moving at a very fast speed up the side of the mountain, and it was loud with an indistinguishable noise. As I approached the very top, the left two lanes had big arrows that curved to the left, and the right two lanes had arrows pointing straight ahead that would lead me over the cliff. I knew in my heart that if I went left, it meant I would be choosing to stay in the relationship with Jason, and there would be more fighting and unrest. I physically felt pain, anguish, and conflict as I looked to the left. However, when I looked straight ahead, I didn't feel or see anything. It was a path towards the unknown. I was moving so fast to the top; I had to quickly decide which direction to take.

Chapter 7

I chose to go straight and flew right off the edge of the cliff at the top of the mountain. I was scared; my stomach dropped, and I couldn't breathe as I started to descend downward into the valley of the mountainous terrain. When I softly landed, it was completely quiet. I was surrounded by views of big beautiful mountains, pastures of brilliant green grass with sparkling streams and rivers throughout the landscape. The sky was clear and blue; the sun was shining so vivid and bright. It was a visually stunning scene. Then I saw me and my son through a window in a light green painted house nearby. We were sitting at a kitchen table inside having a meal. No one else was in the house with us, and he looked to be about 4 or 5 years old. I couldn't tell which meal we were having or what we were talking about; there was just so much peace. We were surrounded by majestic beauty, abundant provision, and great peace.

When I awoke, I knew that not only did I know what decision I wanted and needed to make, but that I had the strength and the backing of the Holy Spirit to make the decision. In that moment, I felt as if I was no longer a broken vessel, but a woman filled with the strength of the Almighty God. I knew that once I made the right decision and had genuine lifestyle repentance, God would take me to this place of beauty and peace. Even as a single mother. I made the decision in my heart, took immediate action that same morning and have been living in a place of abundance and peace from that day forward.

You must continue to pray no matter what your situation or circumstance. God will speak to you in your own special way. It could be with His words, a vision or dream, or a word of wisdom that drops in your spirit. God knows how to get a message to his children. We must be open to receive it. No matter what state we are in, he wants us to talk to him. He wants us to come to him. He wants to be there for you as only He can. As you continue to go to God, wholeheartedly and with transparency, you can receive permanent healing from a broken heart and get to your new place of abundant peace and provision, just as I have. I am still living in that place God showed me. My amazing life where I am surrounded by majestic beauty, abundant provision, and great peace.

Chapter 8

RELEASE THE PAIN

Romans 8:14 New King James Version (NKJV)

For as many as are led by the Spirit of God, these are sons of God.

The Lord has a vision of your healing path specific to your individual circumstance and your uniqueness as a woman. He knows exactly what you need to do to heal and how you need to do it. When Jesus healed in the synoptic gospels, he used various methods and means, yet the end result was always the same: total healing. As you work towards healing your broken heart, allow the Holy Spirit to lead and guide you. He may have unconventional and uncommon methods for you to utilize so that you may receive the total manifestation of your healing.

CREATIVE SELF EXPRESSION TO GET THE PAIN OUT

I am a writer. I have learned that when I am in great pain, writing the pain out is the best way to start receiving expeditious healing. I write publicly in books, blogs, online articles, and downloadable programs, but I also write for my own personal healing through journaling in notes, poems, rhymes, short stories, visions, and dreams. I write list and reminders. The written word is extremely powerful and influential in my life, especially when I am trying to process something whether it's good or bad. If you are a writer, this chapter will give you new ways in which you can write out your pain and receive healing. If you are not a writer, this chapter will inspire you in your own unique area of creativity. Whatever gifts and talents the Lord has given you to help others, you can use them to help yourself in your time of need. It must be a gift or talent that allows for total transparency and unlimited self-expression. Utilizing your gifts expressing thoughts and emotions is a safe and effective outlet to release pain, engage with God and grow closer to him.

When I ended my relationship with my son's father, I was a complete mess spiritually, mentally and emotionally. Months went by, and although I prayed, studied, and went to church, I was still miserable. I had a strong soul tie to him. So strong was the soul tie, that I could literally see a demonic spirit in his form tormenting me daily. Trust me, I know how that sounds, but it's true.

My spirit was broken because I broke a 6-year celibacy walk for the sake of true love. I thought I knew him very well, but I soon realized I did not. I also did not receive any of the love he professed for me; I felt like he literally hated me. I was living in constant guilt, shame, and bitterness. I thought I had forgiven him. I realized that unforgiveness had taken such root in my heart, I couldn't recognize my own hardened heart towards him which had turned into rage. I couldn't control my thoughts, or emotions and I was hormonal. The worst time to face a spiritual battle is when you are pregnant, in my opinion. What you go through directly affects the baby that you are carrying.

I was in this state of torment for my entire pregnancy, although I was making slow progress to breakthrough and healing. The episodes of despair would come and go throughout the months. When I gave birth, I took three months of maternity leave and decided to use the time not only to get into the flow of being a new mom, but to permanently break free from guilt, bitterness, and shame. One day in the midst of an emotional episode, God told me to write my story down. I felt too embarrassed to share all the details with anyone verbally, I barely spoke about what transpired between us with my family and friends. They knew very few details, and most of them were confused about what truly took place between Jason and I. I hid a lot of things from them.

HIDING THE HURT

Hiding the truth and details of an abusive relationship is common for women. We battle with the shame we feel for allowing ourselves to get into those situations, the humiliation from being involved in a situation that was out of our control and trying to protect the man we care about or our own reputation, there is a lot that is hidden. Once we get out of the situation, we still may not have the strength to share all the details of what transpired. Counseling and therapy are extremely helpful and provide a safe space to talk about those things we have hidden in our heart and memory. Counseling is wonderful in the church. However, licensed professional counselors and therapists are trained to help with deeper and more complex issues and wounds. I myself have went through therapy when life issues became too intense and was extremely blessed as a result of participating in therapy. If your church has professional licensed counselors you can speak with, that would be a wonderful resource to help in your healing journey. If not, seek a professional outside of the church. You can even find a professional who has a relationship with Christ, even though they do not attend your church or denomination. Teaching, training, and education into human psychology coupled with the Word of God and the Spirit of God can produce supernatural healing results.

When God told me to write my story down, I tried to figure out how I could write it that would be a blessing to others and still limit my personal humiliation. However, the Lord told me to write all the details down and omit nothing. He revealed to me that one day I might share the story with others, but as for now, this written version of the chain of events was for my own personal healing. I did exactly as I was instructed. I simply wrote, with no format, no plan and no audience in mind. I put all of my story down in narrative form, and I didn't leave any of the ugly details out. It took me about a week to get it typed up. Since I was on maternity leave whenever the baby slept, I wrote. After that week, I felt so much lighter. It was as if a weight had been lifted off of me. At times, I cried as I wrote. Sometimes I had to take long breaks because the memories were too painful and embarrassing. Yet I continued to write as instructed by my Creator. My Father was right. My breakthrough from hurt, bitterness, unforgiveness, and shame all started by first writing my full honest and completely transparent story down, the good, the bad and the ugly.

Fast forward a few years and after the most recent heartbreak took place with John, I had a similar method of writing to get the pain out. Unfortunately, after Reggie and I parted ways, I was not completely healed before I started a relationship with John. After Reggie ended, I knew I needed to help other women by sharing my stories of heartbreak, so I wrote a blog post titled "No More Regrets, No More Fear". It gave a very brief version of what transpired with me and my son's father. However, the blog didn't go deep enough to get me to a place of total healing; it wasn't a full story, just a short narrative with quick tips to help women not live in regret or fear from past decisions. It also didn't speak about what I endured with Reggie. The post was very surface level with little to no details of what took place within the relationship. After John broke my heart, I was completely devastated. As a matter of fact, if I would have healed properly, I may have never entered that relationship. My thinking was still foggy, and my heart was not whole. It was as if the wound was still open, and I allowed John into my heart to love me and make me feel better. But in the end, he ripped that wound apart and created a whole new deeper level of hurt and pain.

This time around I wrote with greater depth and believe that is why I received such permanent healing. One way that I have written is through the transparency of this book. Again, I give the good, the bad and the ugly details. I do not believe in being fake or pretending like I have a perfect godly single woman's walk. I have been tested, and admittedly failed a few times but I am still getting back up and growing with God. This book is created with layers of realness and authenticity for the sake of helping other women like me; imperfect daughters who love their heavenly Father with everything in them.

Another way that I healed through writing in the most recent situation with John was by journaling my random thoughts, instead of calling or texting him. You know how it is. He broke your heart, but you still love him, and you can't seem to pull away. You want to block him from your phone, but you would like him to care, apologize and try to make you feel better. You miss your friendship with him. You may even have more choice words for him. Write it down, instead of reaching out to him. It will make you feel so much better. Get all your thoughts out, the loving thoughts, the hateful thoughts, the hurtful thoughts and even the name calling. I put these all on paper instead of calling him and going off into another ungodly rant. Instead of making myself look foolish or lose my dignity, I journaled. It was so freeing. It feels good to get the pain out instead of holding it all in. It is also better than calling your friends or family and venting time and time again. While you do need their support, when you journal, God can speak directly to you. This avenue of getting the pain out through writing is the best way to heal.

Lastly, I wrote lists, rhymes, and notes to myself. I wrote a list of all the attributes John possessed that were ungodly and unloving so that I could remind myself of who he really was instead of being drawn back in by his personality and manipulation. I wrote a long note to myself as a reminder that he has chosen another woman over me and he never truly loved me. I wrote a rhyme detailing the type of man he was, the type of woman he would rather have in his life and that vengeance was the Lord's, so there was no need for me to try and seek revenge. I wrote what a phone conversation with him would sound like. There was no point in trying to communicate with him any longer, but I still had feelings and thoughts I needed to get out. I got the pain out of my heart and mind by creating these lists, rhymes, and notes for my own healing process.

The written word is very powerful which is why God chose that method of communication to spread the gospel. Even after you have written the pain out, you can read your words out loud which will help to strengthen, encourage and empower

Chapter 9

THE LETTING GO PROCESS

1 Corinthians 6:16 New King James Version (NKJV)

Or do you not know that he who is joined to a harlot is one body with her? For "the two," He says, "shall become one flesh."

A godly soul tie is when a husband and wife have sex, and the two have now become one. An ungodly soul tie occurs when the two have become one through premarital sex outside of a God-ordained marriage covenant. This is why moving on from a breakup, whether you are married and divorcing, or a single person who has had premarital sex, is extremely painful and difficult. Since two souls have been intertwined, they must be severed completely and ripped apart. The process of letting go and moving on is never easy, yet it is possible with the help of the Holy Spirit.

How to Heal a Broken Heart

GETTING HIM OUT OF YOUR SYSTEM

Letting the man or men that hurt you completely go is a process when your heart was completely open to loving them. I believe healing comes permanently through Christ, but we can still have nagging thoughts and desires. We think to ourselves, if he would just come back and do right, maybe we can start over. If he would just sincerely apologize and change his ways, we can have a blessed life together. Well, maybe that will happen because all things are possible through God. However, there is a greater chance that will not actually be the case. I am not trying to dim your faith, but I want to help you face a harsh reality. If that man were good for you, you wouldn't be reading this book trying to heal from what he took you through. If God wanted him to straighten up, he would have done so. If he really loved you the way he professed to, his actions would have been aligned with the actions of godly love. Moving on is hard when your heart is still tugging you backward, but it is not only necessary for your own mental health but imperative for your spiritual growth journey with God.

To get John completely out of my system, I had to stop feeding the monster by talking, texting and checking his social media. An easy way to keep a man in your heart and on your mind, is to keep looking at him, reaching out to him or accepting all his phone calls. Maybe he is calling you to check on how you are doing, or he misses you. John would call because he wanted my advice and guidance or for me to make him laugh. A conversation with John was nice, but it always ended with me double checking whatever he said to me and I always could confirm he was still lying about his side chick turned new girlfriend. Continuing a friendship with him after he broke my heart was not healthy for me. I needed him out of my system completely so that I could stay healed and truly move on with my life. I wanted the door open for the man God has for me, not for John to come back in and break my heart again. I had to block his number and keep him blocked. I had to stay off his social media; I deactivated my Facebook account altogether. I had to stop reaching out to him or rationalizing what I would say the next time he called me. All this behavior only feeds the monster and keeps the hurt and pain alive. It keeps hope alive in a relationship that is clearly dead.

What if you can't end all communication?

If you have children, property, a business or anything that ties you to the man that broke your heart in which you cannot end all communication, hearing from the Lord and obtaining his wisdom is crucial for your healing. When you interact with them, you want the conversations to be focused strictly on the topic at hand to prevent your emotions from spiraling out of control or even getting sucked back into the unhealthy relationship. Similar to a workplace or ministry situation when you have an intense disagreement, yet still have to communicate on a regular basis. Especially if children are involved, you must develop a plan to co-parent as peacefully as possible. Planning in advance how you will engage with them is the best action to take. If you can enlist outside help from your natural or church family, that would be a good option. If that is not possible and you still are unable to find an effective resolution, again I would again recommend counseling, therapy and also life coaching. An outside perspective can help you create the best plan to move forward and maintain peace that is within your control.

During the aforementioned failed relationships and others not contained in this book, I felt as if I had lost myself, emotionally. Therefore, for me to move on and heal, I needed to get back to me, being myself. I changed my complete bed sheet and comforter set and decreed that no man would ever lie in my sheets again, unless it was the husband God has ordained for me and we were married. I also had begun coloring my hair and doing my nails in a way that would please the man I was in a relationship with. I don't mind doing this; I enjoy switching up my style. However, now was a time for me to do what I loved to do best for myself. I dyed my hair jet blue black which is my favorite hair color, and I removed the acrylic nails and got white gel polish only. I took a day off from work and went and got a nice long deep tissue massage. I was already dieting at the tail end of our relationship, so I continued to get my body and health in order by removing bad foods from my diet. I treated myself to some expensive makeup, and I made sure to do things I enjoy with my son daily. On the weekends, I made sure that I didn't just stay in the house, but that we went out to do things that gave me joy and peace. I started reading more articles about potty training and fun activities for toddlers since this was the season of his growth spurt and development. I already planned our yearly vacation trips, but I put those in front me by reviewing my trip details to remind myself of how fun my life would be without John in it. I took the focus off of John and placed my attention on the things I love the most: my baby boy, beauty, and fun.

Additionally, God was showing me how much love I have right now in my life. One night I was thinking about how my phone would not ring because John wouldn't be calling anymore. I had thoughts about lonely nights and how he left me alone while he was cozied up with another woman. Every day that same week a friend or family member called me or stopped by the visit. Some of these friends and family I hadn't spoken to in months. My cousin even told me one day since I miss talking to John so much, just call and talk to him. Although it's not the same, after all, he is my cousin; I was so blessed by his willingness to take care of my need for companionship. I was so amazed at God making my phone ring and showing me that I am not alone at all. Also, when I came to work, I spoke to several of my brothers in Christ who genuinely care about me as a coworker and as a person. Those are safe brotherly relationships with no ulterior motives or intentions. I shared what happened with two of them, and they gave me advice and encouragement that we women need to hear from a strong godly man. They reminded me that I had not lost love, but the pain he caused me was a gain, in that he is not in my life anymore with lies and deceit. From a man's perspective, they could clearly see that nothing was wrong with me, but something is terribly wrong with men who treat women like trash and play toys. Other brothers I work with that I am not so close to had just been noticeably friendlier, and when I felt I was having a weak moment, those small talk conversations helped me not to feed the monster by attempting to communicate with or check up on John. These things will also help you to get the man out of your system and move from a place of pain to a life of great peace.

Lastly, I had to pray for God to break the soul tie that was created through premarital sex. I prayed that God would help me control my thoughts and keep them fixed on the things above, not on the failed relationship. The way you go about breaking a soul tie, most times will involve fasting, prayer and Word-based declarations. I will not go into depth in this book since the focus is not spiritual warfare, but healing. However, spiritual warfare is a part of healing because we do not fight against flesh and blood. I encourage you to find resources regarding spiritual warfare and the breaking of soul ties if this is an area of which you struggle. You can start the process by praying and asking God to completely sever any ties you have to any man in your past that is keeping you bound. You may get free by the power of prayer, as I stated earlier, it is the most powerful thing you can do.

If your heart is broken, God wants you healed and whole, which will require you to get the man who hurt you out of your system. I believe healing comes permanently through Christ and getting the man out of your system and keeping him out is how you maintain your healing.

Chapter 10

ENCOURAGING SCRIPTURES
AND PRAYER FOR HEALING

This book was written with complete honesty and transparency from a place of love. My desire is for my stories to help you not only relate but also encourage you that you can receive total healing and breakthrough. You can use life's lessons of hurt and pain to help others. You can also use these lessons as a stepping stone to help you grow in your faith. Having your heart broken has not broken you forever. You don't have to live your life hurting and confused. Once you are healed, you can emerge with even greater faith and belief in God's love and that he will send you the man of your dreams: a godly husband who understands and walks in the true love of God. These scriptures are the foundation of my healing, and the prayer will assist you in receiving permanent and total healing and deliverance.

How to Heal a Broken Heart

2 Corinthians 12:9 Amplified Bible (AMP)

But He has said to me, "My grace is sufficient for you [My lovingkindness and My mercy are more than enough—always available—regardless of the situation]; for [My] power is being perfected [and is completed and shows itself most effectively] in [your] weakness." Therefore, I will all the more gladly boast in my weaknesses, so that the power of Christ [may completely enfold me and] may dwell in me.

Psalm 147:3 Amplified Bible (AMP)

He heals the brokenhearted and binds up their wounds [healing their pain and comforting their sorrow].

Psalm 34:18 Amplified Bible (AMP)

The Lord is near to the heartbroken and He saves those who are crushed in spirit (contrite in heart, truly sorry for their sin).

Colossians 3:2 Amplified Bible (AMP)

Set your mind and keep focused habitually on the things above [the heavenly things], not on things that are on the earth [which have only temporal value].

Isaiah 61:1-3 Amplified Bible (AMP)

The Spirit of the Lord God is upon me, because the Lord has anointed and commissioned me to bring good news to the humble and afflicted; He has sent me to bind up [the wounds of] the brokenhearted,

To proclaim release [from confinement and condemnation] to the [physical and spiritual] captives and freedom to prisoners, to proclaim [a]the favorable year of the Lord, [b]and the day of vengeance and retribution of our God, To comfort all who mourn,

Chapter 10

To grant to those who mourn in Zion the following: to give them a [c]turban instead of dust [on their heads, a sign of mourning], the oil of joy instead of mourning, the garment [expressive] of praise instead of a disheartened spirit.

So they will be called the trees of righteousness [strong and magnificent, distinguished for integrity, justice, and right standing with God], the planting of the Lord, that He may be glorified.

Matthew 5:44 New King James Version (NKJV)

But I say to you, love your enemies, bless those who curse you, do good to those who hate you, and pray for those who spitefully use you and persecute you,

Hebrews 4:16 Amplified Bible (AMP)

Therefore, let us [with privilege] approach the throne of grace [that is, the throne of God's gracious favor] with confidence and without fear, so that we may receive mercy [for our failures] and find [His amazing] grace to help in time of need [an appropriate blessing, coming just at the right moment].

Prayer for Healing, Peace, and Deliverance

Heavenly Father, I believe that you are Jehovah Rapha the God who heals me. I believe in the healing power of Jesus Christ that lives on the inside of me. I thank you for always being with me and never leaving me to suffer alone. I pray that you will swiftly and completely heal my broken heart and restore me with an abundance of peace and joy. Restore back to me everything that was lost and stolen during this season. I pray that your love would overtake me and I will know and understand your love in a greater capacity. I pray that everything Satan meant for evil, you will turn it around and get the glory from it. Give me wisdom in abundance so that I may know what changes I need to make and how to move forward in this season. Increase my hearing to your voice and make me more sensitive to your Spirit. Continue to draw me closer to you. Allow your healing anointing to flow freely in my life and mend this broken heart and emotions. Help me to move on from all past hurts and pains and to fully forgive those who have hurt me. I release every man into my forgiveness right now and pray that they will have a supernatural encounter with you that would cause them to know and serve Christ with all of their hearts and might. Supernaturally and permanently break every soul tie and kill every fleshly desire that has me bound. I also ask that you restore my faith that you will send me true, lasting and pure love in your perfect timing. Help me not to give up on you or live in doubt and fear, but to trust and believe that your word is true. I thank you for freedom, deliverance and permanent healing in Jesus name, Amen.

About the Author

Sarita A. Foxworth is a certified Christian Life Coach. Her life's work is to help people of God pray, hear from God and obtain the blessed families they desire. She provides biblical prayer based life coaching through group coaching programs, luxury life coaching retreats and global speaking tours.

Her literary works include:

The Single Woman's Prayer Book:
How to Get Answers from Heaven

How to Heal a Broken Heart:
Transition from Pain to Peace

How to Prepare for Your Future Husband:
Waiting, Dating and Trusting God for Your Adam

Giving Birth to Miracles:
Manifesting Supernatural Childbirth

The Prophetic Woman:
Boldly Declaring the Word of the Lord

"My goal is to help you to hear from God, flow with God and manifest what he desires for your life"- *Sarita A. Foxworth*

To book Sarita as a guest speaker at your next event visit

www.Saritafoxworth.com

and fill out the contact us form. To attend a live online or in person event join Sarita's mailing list.

Printed in Great Britain
by Amazon

82364106R00051